TANDEM

There Was a Young Lady

Hugh De Witt

The bawdiest verse form in the English
language, the limerick has been a source
of ribald delight for over a hundred
years. This collection contains more than
four hundred of the best and bawdiest,
including many that have never been
published before.

There Was a Young Lady

Hugh De Witt

TANDEM
33 Beauchamp Place, London, SW3

First published in Great Britain by
Universal-Tandem Publishing Co Ltd, 1969
Reprinted 1969

Made and printed in Great Britain by
The Garden City Press Limited,
Letchworth, Hertfordshire

FOREWORD

FOR well over a century the five-line nonsense verse called the limerick has delighted great numbers of people throughout the English-speaking world. There can be few men in Britain who do not know by heart (even unwillingly) at least half a dozen limericks, and the number must be legion who have attempted to contribute at least one limerick to the national repertory.

About its origin, no certain answer can be given. There are those who say that "limerick" is a corruption of "Learick". Certainly, Edward Lear (London born of Danish descent) it was who popularized the limerick with publication of his *Book of Nonsense* in 1846. But in 1821, in London, there had been published *The History of Sixteen Wonderful Old Women*, and in the following year appeared another collection of nonsense verse called *Anecdotes and Adventures of Fifteen Gentlemen*. Both sets are similar to the Lear pattern. Even here we are unlikely to have the origin.

The *Oxford English Dictionary* gives the probable origin as a party game popular in Ireland in the eighteenth century, in which each member in turn of a "convivial group" would extemporize on nonsense themes concerning men and women from Irish towns, closing with the the chorus: "Will you come up to Limerick?"

Langford Reed, a keen collector of limericks, has suggested that soldiers of the Irish Brigade, organized in the city of Limerick in 1691, brought back from France a decade or two later a type of five-line verse popular in that country. The themes were either religion or nursery rhymes, including:

Digere, Digere, Doge,
La souris ascend l'horloge;
L'horloge frappe,
La souris s'échappe,
Digere, Digere, Doge.

Which rings a bell even if one does not know a word of French.

The *Encyclopaedia Britannica* pours cold water on both these theories, pointing out that the extemporized nonsense of the party game bore little resemblance to the limerick as we know it. Nor do they think much of *Dickery, Dickery, Dock* as an early limerick.

Yet the nursery rhyme in general is the probable key. Lear composed his nonsense verses for the entertainment of the children of his friend the Earl of Derby, and he said that his model was the nursery rhyme *The Old Man of Tobago*.* This appeared in James Orchard Halliwell's book *The Nursery Rhymes of England* (1842), in which he included only rhymes familiar in the eighteenth century or earlier. Nearly half of the known English nursery rhymes are more than two hundred years old. Some scholars believe that some nursery rhymes are thousands of years old— Humpty Dumpty, for instance.

The limerick has marked affinities with the nursery rhyme : its regular rhythm, its rhyme, its nonsense, its immediacy of appeal, and its power to stay in the memory. Sir Thomas Beecham used to say that good music was "that which penetrates the mind with facility and leaves the memory with difficulty". The same could be said of the good limerick.

Lear could not have foreseen the craze the limerick was to become. Its Golden Age was in late-Victorian and Edwardian times, reaching its peak of creativity around 1907/8 when the competition craze was at its

The Old Man of Tobago is mentioned by Charles Dickens in the second chapter of *Our Mutual Friend*.

height. On July 17, 1908, the House of Commons was told that the sale of sixpenny postal orders in Britain had risen from the normal figure of 700,000 to 800,000 for the previous six months to a staggering 11,400,000. The reason was the limerick competitions run by a number of journals for which the entry fee was sixpence an attempt, usually to complete the missing last line of a limerick. The limerick became big business. Publishers of rhyming dictionaries were suddenly seen to be mixing with the social set and holidaying abroad. There were trade journals, giving details of competitions. Books were written on how to win limerick prizes, and one could make a good living by calling oneself "professor" and offering for sale last lines for current competitions.

But, except during this competition-craze period, the main bulk of limerick composition, and also by far the *best* limericks, have been that orally-circulated kind sometimes referred to as "the Stock Exchange variety". This may, or may not, be an apt description, but certainly they are known and enjoyed wherever men without women are to be found : in the Army, Navy, and Air Force, in offices and factories, in colleges and universities. They are popular entertainment at stag parties and at rugby and other sporting club dinners. The ribald limerick has been a British tradition for well over a century and a safety-valve in a society in which Puritan attitudes and taboos have been a long time dying.

As such, it is an interesting facet of our culture and one that awaits psychological and sociological study. Part of that study would be to investigate the regional popularity of the limerick. My own limited investigation confirms what one would expect : that the chief British centres for the limerick are in Scotland, Wales, Ireland, and the northern counties of England, i.e. those areas where Victorian attitudes have been most strongly entrenched. An American friend confirms a similar position in his country.

The content of the limerick has remained inviolate for well over a century. It cocks a snook at "respectable" *mores*. The pompous, the prudish, the stuffy, the snobbish, and the hypocritically pious are taken down a peg or four.

Cocking a snook at authority begins at school, when the limerick-like jingle becomes an instrument of rebellion and impropriety. The target is the school-teacher, the parson, the policeman.

English schoolkids in the cities sometimes taunt the policeman on his beat with:

> There's a copper on his beat,
> You can smell his cheesy feet,
> There's a copper over there.

Bawdiness creeps in well before puberty. For half a century or more London's cockney kids have been chanting a jingle which runs:

> I got a girl in Waterloo,
> She don't wear no — yes, she do!
> I got a girl in Leicester Square,
> She don't wear no underwear.

Children seem in psychological need of moments of impropriety. Iona and Peter Opie, leading collectors of nursery rhymes, see the parody of these verses as an intelligent child's way of showing independence without serious or destructive rebellion.

A favourite improper parody of this kind is of *Mary Had a Little Lamb*, one verse of which goes:

> Mary had a little lamb
> She fed it castor oil.
> And everywhere the lamb would go,
> It fertilized the soil.

One suspects, too, that class factors come into it—as in those delightful limericks in which the anonymous

8

versifier scores game, set, and match in verbal encounters with the aristocracy. The recurring ironic use of the word "lady" surely has social significance; also the frequent use of the vocabulary of the "upper class"— "jolly", "rather", "exceedingly". Note that it was a "low fellow" who shouted "Beaver!" at Lady Godiva (165).

Members of the aristocracy—also the Church—behave with startling impropriety, though usually retaining their stylized manner of speaking. Though in the grip of strong emotion, good manners do not forsake the guest who exclaims to a hostess: "How appealing! May I piss in the fire?" A commoner fellow would not have bothered to ask (301).

The bawdy popular jingle was a feature of British life for several centuries before Lear. In the eighteenth century—the great hey-day of British bawdiness—a profusion of ribald verse was composed about leading politicians, aristocrats, courtesans, and entertainers. An account of this rumbustious period, entertaining on every page, has been given by Jack Loudan in his book *The Hell Rakes*,* which quotes many bawdy jingles of the day.

The four Georges did not escape the satire, and there is yet another link with nursery rhymes in the belief that the original *Georgie Porgie* was in fact George I. On page 58 of Jack Loudan's book is a verse in limerick form:

> The beautiful Peg who showed such a leg,
> When lately she dressed in men's clothes.
> A creature uncommon
> Who's both man and woman,
> The chief of the belles and the beaux.

The victim here was the actress Peg Woffington. These were the times when one could have an epitaph such as this:

*Available from Universal-Tandem Publishing Co.

> HERE LIES TWO POOR LOVERS
> WHO HAD THE MISHAP
> THOUGH VERY CHASTE PEOPLE
> TO DIE OF THE CLAP

The limerick often tells a cruel or disgusting story. Yet the normal reaction is neither horror nor disgust, but amusement. Why is this? A similar question could be asked of the nursery rhyme, whose plot would be horrific in any other form. (Try telling nursery rhyme stories or limericks in straight prose!)

The answer lies in the nonsense and fantasy which disengage our emotions, except those of amusement and delight. We do not cry for *Humpty Dumpty* any more than we feel pity for Lear's unfortunate old man:

> There was an old man who screamed out
> Whenever they knocked him about.
>   So they took off his boots
>   And fed him on fruits.
> And continued to knock him about.

It is all such obvious nonsense and make-believe that our normal reactions of horror and compassion are not aroused.

It is clear that the limerick, like the nursery rhyme, appeals to some need deep in the human psyche—but readers will wish to enjoy the limericks of this anthology without being overconcerned with psychological or sociological motivations and undertones. Though the ingredients just described are undoubtedly present, the limerick could not have sustained its appeal for so long but for other stronger assets.

Not the least important of these is its roistering rhythm and clever rhyming. The music of phrase and rhyme dances in the mind and stays in the memory as vividly as the nursery rhymes one heard in childhood. The best limericks have the instant appeal of the popular tune.

Word-play and rhyming are often ingenious. Sometimes there are rhyming volleys, which excite the ear like the brief but fierce rat-a-tat of experts doubles players volleying close in at the net. And, like the spectators at the tennis match, we applaud, inwardly.

But the chief ingredient of the limerick is its nonsensical humour. Succinctly, often using mainly monosyllabic words, a zany picture is conjured up before the mind's eye, triggering off instant upheavals of diaphragm and abdominal viscera that can only be health-enhancing and invigorating.

The humour is that of incongruity and surprise. Often, as in an O.Henry short story, the surprise comes in the last line. The first four lines may build up a reasonable picture, but already we are smiling in anticipation of the bizarre twist but seconds away. It may even come on the final note, like the Italian tenor's climatic high C. One could be let down—but it is surprising how rarely this happens. The percentage of winning limericks is high.

Other limericks are incident packed to a miraculous degree, like students piling into an old car to set some crazy record—so that the reading, taking only a few seconds, becomes fraught with danger for the laughter-ribs.

Finally, it is often overlooked that the humble limerick can be very good poetry indeed. Norman Douglas it was who pointed out that "I sat with the Duchess at tea" (37) is one of the most perfect examples of English poetry to be found. There are others as good—beautifully concise and compact. They tell a story, or make a point, with maximum effectiveness, using a minimum of words.

In short : the good limerick delights the ear, wins our admiration, appeals to our sense of fantasy and nonsense, evokes immediate laughter, and has a dash of Rabelaisian gusto that releases tensions.

Of course, the ribald limerick is not for squeamish

and oversensitive souls like that fragile lady who fainted away at the sight of canary manure (149) or the other who blenched at the sound of a chain being pulled in a neighbouring room (97). But supporters of the limerick—a considerable army—believe its honest vulgarity to be bracingly wholesome, like that of its near relation, the comic seaside postcard. Belly laughter is just about the most therapeutic activity there is.

A few brief points to conclude this foreword.

Though this is by far the largest collection of limericks of this kind to be published in Britain, not a few are sure to have escaped the net. My apologies if this includes any favourites of the reader.

This collection is composed of the traditional repertory, orally collected but matched with and reinforced by some old anthologies, plus a considerable number of hitherto unpublished verses. Many of the orally collected limericks were inferior variants of originals; but included are variants which seem either to better or match the original version.

Considering that the bulk of the repertory was composed nearly a century ago, the wonder is not that variants exist, but that word-perfect originals are still commonly heard.

No attempt has been made to classify or group limericks under headings. This, I am sure, leads to monotony. Rather, in what may seem at first glance an arbitrary arrangement, have I sought for variety and contrast.

One last point : like other anthologies of verse, this book is not for devouring in large helpings, however tempted one might be, but is rather for savouring, a few stanzas at a time, perhaps occasionally for memorizing—and, I hope, for enjoying, not now and again, but NOW and again and again and AGAIN.

HUGH DE WITT

1

There was a young lady of Onger,
Who got into bed with a conger.
   When asked how it felt,
   She replied: "Though it smelt,
It was just like a man, only longer."

2

An hoary old monk of North China
Once said: "There is nothing diviner
   Than to sit in one's cell
   And let one's mind dwell
On the charms of a virgin vagina."

3

There was an old buffer of Bath,
Who showed girls his J.T. for a laugh.
   You will probably think
   He had too much to drink—
But t'was only a way that he hath.

4

A conductor, Abner McFuss,
Liked to fondle young boys on his bus;
   Then go out and sniff ****s
   And the assholes of birds—
He sure was a funny old cuss.

5

There was a young lady named Myrtle,
Who was both attractive and fertil:
   She would say: "Please stay still,
   Till I've swallowed my Pill!"
Such a sensible lady was Myrtle.

6

There was a young man of Toledo,
Who was cursed with excessive libido:
   To **** and to screw,
   And to fornicate too,
Were the three major planks of his credo,

7

"I am the Bishop of Ardleigh,[1]
And though you mightn't think it of me,
  I've a face like a lamb,
  A ***** like a ram,
And a mind like a W.C."

8

An anaemic young lady from Stoke,
Who in favour of chastity spoke,
  By her doctor was told:
  "If I may make so bold,
What you need is a jolly good poke."

9

There is an old man of Uttoxeter,
Who curses his wife and throws socks at her;
  When she dares to complain,
  (I say this with pain),
By waving his **** he just mocks at her.

10

A young fancy boy of Khartoum
Took a Lesbian up to his room
    But they argued all night
    As to who had the right
To do what, with which, and to whom.

11

Then up spake a Prince of Siam:
"For women I don't give a damn.
    They haven't the grip,
    Nor the velvety tip,
Nor the scope of the assholes of man."

12

There was a young girl from Rantage,
Of whom the Town Clerk took advantage.
    The Borough Surveyor
    Said: "I think you should pay her;
You've altered the whole of her frontage."

13

There was a young gentleman from Grant,
Who was rather a sensitive plant.
When asked: "Do you ****?"
He replied: "No such luck!
I would, if I could—but I can't."

14

A scraggy old spinster of Bude
Said: "Men are exceedingly rude.
When I bathe in the sea,
They all follow me,
To see my pudenda protrude."

15

There was a young man of Montrose,
Who could diddle himself with his toes.
He did it so neat,
He fell in love with his feet,
And christened them Myrtle and Rose.

16

There was a young lady of Dee,[2]
Who went down the river to pee:
   A man in a punt
    Put his hand on her ****,
And God! how I wish it was me.

17

There was a young man from the Coombe,
Who was born six months too soon.
   He hadn't the luck
    To be got from a ****,
But a toss-off shoved in with a spoon.

18

There was a young plumber of Lee,[3]
Who was plumbing a girl by the sea.
   When she said: "Someone's coming!"
   He replied (while still plumbing):
"If anyone's coming, it's me!"

19

There was a young lady of Gloucester
Met a passionate fellow who tossed her.
   She wasn't much hurt,
   But he dirtied her skirt—
Oh! think of the anguish it cost her.

20

Then up spake the King of Siam:
"For women I don't give a damn;
   But a fat-bottomed boy
   Is my pride and my joy—
They call me a bugger: *I am*!"

21

There was a young maiden of Bonely,
Whom the men never let feel lonely;
   So she hung out in front
   Of her popular ****
A sign reading: STANDING ROOM ONLY.

22

A bawdy young rake from Tashkent
Had a ***** that was horribly bent;
   To get over the trouble,
   He pushed it in double—
And instead of his coming, he went.

23

There once was a son-of-a-bitch,
Neither clever, nor handsome, nor rich;
   Yet the girls he would dazzle,
   And **** to a frazzle,
Then ditch them, the son-of-a-bitch.

24

There was a young lady of Harwich,
Who said on the eve of her marriage:
   "I shall sew my chemise
   Right down to my knees,
For I'm damned if I'll **** in the carriage."

25

Said the Reverend Jabez McCotten:
"Sex of the Devil's begotten."
   Said Jones to Miss Bly:
   "Never mind the old guy;
To the pure almost everything's rotten."

26

In the Garden of Eden lay Adam,
Complacently stroking his madam;
   Very loud was his mirth
   For on all of the earth
There were only two ****s—*and he had 'em.*

27

There was a young lady of Malta,
Who strangled her aunt with a halter.
   She said: "I won't bury her,
   She'll do for my terrier—
She'll keep for a month if I salt her."

28

A dirty old man of Madrid
Cast lewd eyes on a plump-bottomed kid.
   Said he : "Oh, what joy !
   I'll ****** that boy.
You see if I don't"—*and he did.*

29

There were three girls of Twickenham,
Who loved to have student's ***** in 'em.
   They knelt on the sward
   And prayed to the Lord
To lengthen and strengthen and thicken 'em.

30

Then up spake the Bey of Algiers :
"I am old and well stricken with years.
   And my language is blunt ;
   But a **** is a ****,
And ****ing is ****ing—(*Loud cheers*).

31

There was an old lady of Bermuda,
Who shot a marauding intruder.
   It was not her ire
   At his lack of attire,
But his grabbing her jewels as he *****ed her.

32

When the Bermondsey bricklayers struck,
Bill Bloggins was 'avin' a ****;
   By union rules
   'e 'ad to down tools—
Now wasn't that 'ard bleedin' luck?

33

A randy *tenore robusto*
Chases the women *con gusto*:
   In the middle of *Faust*,
   (I admit, he was soused),
He joggled the soprano's *bel busto*.

34

There was a young lady named Nelly,
Whose tits could be joggled like jelly.
    They could tickle her ****,
     Or be tied in a knot—
They could even swat flies on her belly.[34]

35

There was a young lady of Brussels,
Who was proud of her vaginal muscles:
    She could easily plex them
     And so interflex them
As to whistle love songs through her bustles.

36

In a hammock a fellow named Bliss
Was ****ing a cautious young miss.
    She wriggled and squirmed
     So as not to get spermed
And ended up something like this.

37

I sat with the Duchess at tea,[5]
Who asked: "Do you fart when you pee?"
  I said: "Not a bit
  Do you belch when you ****?"
And felt this was one up for me.

38

There was a young fellow named Fort,
Whose *****, although thick, was quite short;
  But to make up for the loss
  He had ****s like a hoss
And he never shot less than a quart.

39

There was a young virgin of Dover,
Who was raped in the woods by a drover.
  When the going got hard
  He greased her with lard,
Which felt nice, so they started all over.

40

A voyeur was caught in the dark as
He spied on erotic car-parkers;[6]
    But when told to desist
    Said : "I just can't resist
Couples who lark when they are starkers."

41

There was a young girl of Baroda,
Who built a remarkable pagoda :
    The walls of its halls
    Were hung with the ****s
and the ****s of the fools that bestrode her.

42

A wonderful tribe are the Sweenies,
Renowned for the length of their peenies.
    The hair on their *****
    Sweeps the floors in their halls,
But they don't look at women—the meanies !

43

There was a young lady named Sue,
Who preferred a stiff drink to a screw.
 But one leads to the other,
 And now she's a mother—
Let this be a lesson to *you*.

44

There was a young man from Cornell,
Who said: 'I'm aware of a smell;
 But whether it's drains
 Or human remains,
I'm really unable to tell."

45

There was a young man of Seattle,
Whose testicles tended to rattle.
 He said, as he ****èd
 Some stones in a bucket:
"If Stravinsky don't deafen you—that'll."

46

There was a young girl of East Lynne,
Whose mother, to save her from sin,
   Had filled up her ****
   With shellac to the brim—
But the boys picked it out with a pin.

47

Said Oscar McDingle O'Figgle,
With an almost hysterical giggle:
   "Last night I was sick
   With delight when my *****
Felt dear Alfred's delicious ass wriggle!"

48

There was a young girl named Heather,
Whose **** was made of leather.
   She made an odd noise
   For attracting the boys
By flapping the edges together.

49

Then up spake a Hindu mahout:
"What's all this bletherin' about?
    Why, I spend my *****
    Up an elephant's trunk"—
(*Cries of* "Shame! He's a ****! Throw him
    out!")

50

A two-balled old man of Arbroath
Gave vent to a terrible oath;
    When one chanced to ache,
    By an awful mistake,
A keen surgeon chopped off them both.

51

There was an old lady of Ealing,
Who had a peculiar feeling—
    She lay on her back,
    Threw wide open her *****,
And pissed from the floor to the ceiling.

52

There was a young fellow named Bliss,
Whose sex life was sadly amiss;
   For even with Venus
   His recalcitrant penis
Could never do better than t
                        h
                        i
                        s

53

Regardez-vous Toulouse-Lautrec?
At first glance an ambulent wreck.
   He could **** once a week
   A la maniere antique,
And once in a while *à la Grecque.*

54

There was a young girl from Hong Kong,
Whose cervical cap was a gong.
   She said, with a yell,
   As a shot rang the bell:
"I'll give you a ding for a dong."

55

There was a young fellow of Natal,
And Sue was the name of his gal.
    All the way over
     From Durban to Dover
He was passing through Suez Canal.

56

Then up spake the Bey of Algiers,
To his harem he said : "My dears,
    You may think it odd o'me,
     But I've given up sodomy—
Tonight there'll be ****ing !—(*loud cheers*).

57

There was an old woman of Thrace,
Whose nose spread all over her face.
    She had very few kisses :
     The reason for this is—
There wasn't a suitable place.

58

A brawny young athlete named Grimmon,
Who developed a new way of swimmin':
    By a marvellous trick,
    He could scull with his *****,
Which attracted loud cheers from the women.

59

There was a young lady named Rose,
With erogenous zones in her toes.
    She remained onanistic
    'Till a foot-fetichistic
Young man became one of her beaux.

60

There was a young man of Ostend,[7]
Whose wife caught him ****ing her friend.
    "It's no use, my duck,
    Interrupted her ****,
For I'm damned if I draw till I spend."

61

There was a young girl of Antigua,
Whose mother said: "Mabel, how bigua."
    Mabel said: "What?
    Do you refer to my ****?
My bum, belly-button, or figua?"

62

There was a young man of Cape Horn,
Who wished he had never been born:
    And he would not have been
    If his father had seen
That the end of the sheath was torn.

63

There once was a spinster of Ealing,
Endowed with such delicate feeling,
    That she thought that a chair
    Should not have its legs bare—
So she kept her eyes fixed on the ceiling.

64

There was a young man of Delray,
Who ******ed his father one day.
   Said he: "I like rather
   To stuff it up father.
He's clean and there's nothing to pay."

65

The girl Up The Junction was mad,
For trade was unusually bad;
   Since the place had won fame,
   It had lost its good name,
And the hippies had made it *their* pad.

66

There was an old fellow named West,
Whose John T. came up to his chest.
   He said: "I declare
   I have no pubic hair"—
So he covered his ***** with his vest.

67

Said a pretty young whore of Hong Kong
To a long-prongèd patron named Wong:
   "They say my vagina's
   The sweetest in China—
Don't spoil it by donging it wrong."

68

There was a young man from Rheims,
Who at night had one hundred wet dreams.
   By a stroke of pure wit,
   He got covered with ****,
But sold them as chocolate creams.

69

A nice old lady named Carey
Suspected her son was a fairy.
   "It's peculiar," said she.
   "He sits down to pee
And stands when I bathe the canary."

70

A widow who lived in Rangoon
Hung a black-ribboned wreath on her womb,
   "To remind me," she said,
   "Of my husband who's dead,
And of what put him into his tomb."

71

An Irish girl born at Stillorgan
Had a Welsh music master called Morgan.
   He taught her the lute
   And she played on his flute—
But the thing she liked best was his organ.

72

There was a young fellow, a banker,
Who had bubo, itch, pox, and chancre.
   He got all four
   From a dirty old whore—
So he wrote her a letter to thank her.

73

There was a young lady of Cheam,
Who crept into a vestry unseen.
   She pulled down her knickers,
   Likewise the vicar's,
And said : "How about it, old bean?"

74

A strange young fellow from Kent
Was famed wherever he went :
   All the way through a ****,
   He would quack like a duck,
Then crow like a cock as he spent.

75

Then up spake the King of Spain :
"To **** and to bugger is pain ;
   But it's quite *infra dig*
   On occasion to frig—
Yet I do it again and again."

76

There was a young lady named Myrtle,
Who had an affair with a turtle.
    She had crabs, so they say,
    In nine months to a day—
Which proves that the turtle was fertil'.

77

There was a young plumber of Lee,
Who was getting his H-O-L-E.
    When she said: "Someone's coming,"
    He carried on plumbing,
Saying: "You're right, my dear—it's *me*!"

78

There was a young girl of Djakarta,[8]
Who was widely acclaimed as a farter:
    At the African sports
    Her deafening reports
Brought her great fame as a starter.

79

A nervous young fellow named Fred
Took a charming young widow to bed.
    When he'd diddled a while
    She remarked with a smile:
"You've got in all in 'cept the head."

80

There was a young girl from Siberia,
Whose morals were grossly inferior.
    She slept with a nun,
    Which she shouldn't have done—
And now she's a Mother Superior.

81

There was a faith-healer of Deal,[9]
Who said: "Although pain isn't real,
    When sometimes by chance
    I shoot in my pants,
I dislike what I fancy I feel."

82

A hermit who had an oasis
Thought it the best of all places.
 He could pray and be calm
 'Neath a pleasant date-palm,
While lice on his genitals ran races.[10]

83

There was a young girl of Asturias
With a penchant for practices curious.
 She loved to bat rocks
 With her gentlemen's ****s—
A practice both rude and injurious.[11]

84

An organist playing at York
Had a ***** that could hold a small fork,
 And between obligatos
 He'd munch at tomatoes,
To keep up his strength while at work.

85

A young lady from far Samarkand
Attempted to dance nude in the Strand.
   The policeman on duty
   Said : "No, me proud beauty ;
Them foreign contortions is banned."

86

There was a young student of St. John's,[12]
Who wanted to ****** the swans.
   Conscientious hall porter :
   "Pray, take my daughter !
The swans are reserved for the dons."

87

There was a young lady who said,
As her husband got into the bed :
   "I'm tired of the stunt
   That you do with my ****,
Why not try my bottom instead."

88

The noble young Lord Godfrey Killasis
Was a sad case of satyriasis,
    Till help psychiatric
    Brought this ****ing fanatic
To a reasonable sexual stasis.

89

Most girls of sexy proportions
Now take contraceptive precautions:
    But young Ermyntrude
    Let a small sperm intrude:
You know a good man for abortions?

90

There was a young student of Trinity,
Who shattered his sister's virginity.
    He made love to his brother,
    Gave twins to his mother,
Yet won highest honours in Divinity.

91

There was a young lady named Hopper,
Who came a society cropper.
    She went to Ostend,
    With a gentleman friend—
The rest of the story's improper.

92

A maestro directing in Rome
Had a quaint way of driving it home.
    Whoever he climbed
    Had to keep her tail timed
To the beat of his old metronome.

93

There was a young girl of Detroit,
Who at ****ing was truly adroit:
    To a pin-point or finer,
    She could squeeze her vagina,
Or open it out like a quoit.

94

There was a young boy of Peru,[13]
Who found he had nothing to do.
   So he sat on the stairs
   And counted pubic hairs,
Saying: "I reckon I have twenty-two."

95

There was a young woman of Maine,
Who openly pissed in the train.
   Not once, but again,
   And again, and again,
And again, and again, and AGAIN!

96

A randy old bishop of Birmingham
Deflowered young girls whilst confirming 'em.
   Midst encouraging applause,
   He'd pull off their drawers
And inject episcopal sperm in 'em.

97

A lacklustre lady of Brougham[14]
Weaved all night at her loom:
   Anon she doth blench
When her lord and his wench
Pull a chain in a neighbouring room.

98

A robust young fellow named Lear
Used to cold sitz his ******** with beer.
   Said he: "By ye gods,
   This is good for the cods—
And should lengthen my ****ing career."

99

There was a young girl from the Creek,
Who had periods three times a week.
   "How very provoking,"
   Said the vicar, near choking,
"There's no time for poking, so to speak."

100

A Scot from the town of Dundee
Wore his kilts rather high from the knee ;
   Of course, you conclude,
   It was frightfully rude,
But his mother still dresses him—See?

101

There was a young girl of Kilkenny,
Whose usual charge was a penny.
   But for half of that sum
   Her round rosy bum
Was a source of amusement to many.

102

There was a young man from Westminster,
Whose designs were base and sinister.
   His lifelong ambition
   Was anal coition
With the wife of a cabinet minister.

103

A certain young sheik I'm not namin'
Asked a flapper he thought he was tamin':
 "Have you a maidenhead?"
 "Don't be foolish!" she said,
"But I still have the box that it came in."

104

The Archbishop pressed, to his breast, undressed,
The wife of the Vicar of Bray.
 She said: "It is rude
 To be lewd in the nude"—
So he put on his old school tay.

105

There was a young girl named Priscilla,
Who flavoured her **** with vanilla.
 The taste was so fine
 Men and beasts stood in line,
Including a stud armadillo.

106

There was a young student of Oriel,
Who flouted the ruling proctorial.
   He ran down the Corn
   With a hell of a horn
And ******ed the Martyrs's Memorial.

107

There was a young girl of Tralee,
Whose knowledge of French was "Oui, oui."
   When she was asked: "****ez-vous?"
   She replied: "And up you!"—
She was famed for her bright repartee.

108

There was a young man of Missouri,
Who ****ed with a terrible fury;
   Till hauled up to court
   For his bestial sport,
And condemned by a poorly-hung jury.

109

At a high Tory rally at Kew,
Wearing Union Jack briefs of bright hue,
   A girl, committing bad form,
   Spread her knees on the platform.
Heckler: "Down with the red, white, and blue!"

110

There was an old fellow of Ealing,
Devoid of all delicate feeling:
   When he read, on the door,
   "Don't spit on the floor,"
He inverted and **** on the ceiling.

111

A young girl was married in Chedder;
Her mother she kissed and she blessed her.
   Said she: "You're in luck,
   He's a rattling good ****,
For I had him myself once in Leicester."

112

The latest reports from Cape Hope
State that apes there have ****** thick as rope,
   And **** high, wide and free,
   From the top of one tree
To the top of the next—what a scope!

113

There was a young priest of Dundee,
Who went back of the parish to pee.
   He said: *"Pax vobiscum,*
   Why doesn't the piss come?
I must have the C-L-A-P!"[15]

114

A charming young lady named Pat
Would invite one to do this and that.
   When speaking of this,
   She meant more than a kiss:
So imagine her meaning of that!

115

There was an old monk of Lahore,
Whose ***** was a yard long or more;
    So he wore the damn thing
    In a surgical sling
To keep it from wiping the floor.

116

There was a young woman of Cheadle,
Who once gave the clap to a beadle.
    Said she: "Does it itch?"
    "It does, you damn bitch,
And burns like hell fire when I peedle."

117

There once was a young fellow from Wick,
Whose John T. was remarkably thick;
    But he took a young bride,
    Whose front door was so wide
That they easily managed the trick.

118

There was a young harlot of Yale,
Whose price-list was tattooed on her tail,
    And on her behind,
    For aid of the blind,
She had REDUCTIONS FOR PARTIES in Braille.

119

"Speak clearly," said he, "roll your r's,"
As he lectured the young curates' class.
    "Dean," said one in reply,
    "To speak clearly I'll try,
But why must I waggle my ****?"

120

There was a young girl named Louise
With a marvellous vaginal squeeze.
    She inspired such pleasure
    In her lover's yard measure
That she caused his untimely decease.

121

Said His Worship: "Now, Mary O'Morgan,
Did the prisoner uncover his organ?"
   Said Mary: "I'm not sure,
   I've not seen one before—
But 'twas more like a flute than an organ."

122

There once was a pretty young miss,
Who loved watching her lover piss.
   She made him drink water
   Much more than he oughter,
And lager assured her of bliss.

123

A mortician who practised in Fife
Made love to the corpse of his wife.
   "How could I know, Judge?
   She was cold, didn't budge—
Just the same as she'd acted in life."

124

There was a young maid of Ostend,
Who swore she'd hold out to the end;
    But alas! half way over
    Twixt Calais and Dover,
She did what she didn't intend.

125

There once was a dentist named Bone,
Who saw all his patients alone.
    In a fit of depravity
    He filled the wrong cavity—
But my, how his practice has grown!

126

Said a forward young damsel of Dijon
To her timorous swain: "Why, you're shy, John.
    Since at billing and cooing
    There's not very much doing,
Do you mind if I undo your fly, John?"

127

A worried young man from Stamboul
Discovered red rings on his ****.
    Said the doctor (a cynic):
    "Get out of my clinic!
Just wipe off the lipstick, you fool!"

128

There was a young maid of Asturias,
Whose temper was frantic and furious.
    She used to throw figs
    At gentlemen's *****—
A habit unpleasant, but curious.

129

There was an old fellow of Gosham,
Who took out his ******** to wash 'em.
    His wife said: "Now, Jack,
    If you don't put them back,
I'll step on your scrotum and squash 'em."

130

A stockbroker, with twinkling eyes,
When asked what was likely to rise,
    Said : "Send in young Winnie
    In thigh-showing minnie,
And then keep your eyes on the flies."

131

There was a young lady whose joys
Were achieved with incomparable poise.
    She could have an orgasm
    With never a spasm—
She could fart without making a noise.

132

There was a young man of Coblenz,
Whose ******** were simply immense :
    It took forty-four draymen,
    A priest and three laymen,
To carry them thither and thence.

133

There was a young lady of Eccles,
Whose **** was covered with freckles.
   But the boys didn't mind,
   For she made a good grind,
And she did it for love and not shekels.

134

Asked what she desired most of all,
"A penis," said a woman of Gaul.
   Her husband said: "No,
   It is not pronounced so.
They say 'appiness, I recall."

135

There was a young couple named Kelly,
Who had to live belly to belly;
   Because once in their haste
   They used library paste
Instead of petroleum jelly.

136

There once was a heathen Chinee,
Who went out in the backyard to pee.
   Said he: "What is thisee?
   My *****ee no pissee.
Hellee! Damnee! Buggeree!"

137

There was a young parson named Binns,
Who talked about women and things;
   But his secret desire
   Was a boy in the choir
With a bottom like jelly on springs.

138

There was a young dancer of Ipswich,
Who took most astonishing skips, which
   So delighted a miss
   She said: "Give us a kiss!"
He replied: "On the cheeks or the lips, which?"

139

There was a young girl from Madrid,
Who found she was having a kid.
    They fed her on rubber,
    On strings and on blubber:
She gave birth to a Dunlop—nonskid!

140

A young lady in Kalamazoo
Once strolled after dark by the zoo.
    She was seized by the nape,
    And raped by an ape
And she murmured: "A wonderful screw."

141

There was a young lady named Prentice,
Who had an affair with a dentist.
    To make the thing easier
    He used anaesthesia,
And *****ed her *non compos mentis.*

142

There was a young lady of Bude,
Who was so meticulously prude,
   She pulled down the blind
   When changing her mind,
Lest some passer-by should intrude.

143

A psychoneurotic fanatic
Said : "I take young girls to my attic,
   Then whistle a tune
   'Bout the cow and the moon—
When the cow jumps, I come. It's dramatic!"

144

A fantastic young prince of Sirocco
Had erotical penchants rococo.
   The ***** of this Prince
   Was flavoured with quince
And he seasoned his semen with cocoa.

145

There was a young girl from Dundee,
Who was raped by an ape up a tree.
    The result it was horrid—
    All ass and no forehead,
Three ***** and a purple goatee.

146

A bibulous bishop would preach
After sunning his ***** on the beach;
    But his love life was ended
    By a paunch so distended
It annulled, *ipso facto,* his reach.

147

There was a young lady called Alice,
Who peed in a Catholic chalice.
    She said: "I do this
    From a great need to piss,
And not from sectarian malice."

148

There was a young man of Bengal,
Who went to a fancy-dress ball.
   Just for a whim,
   He went as a ****
And was had by a dog in the hall.

149

A fragile old lady called Muir
Had a mind so exquisitely pure
   That she fainted away
   At a friend's house one day
When she saw some canary manure.

150

There was a young seedsman of Leeds,
Who swallowed six packets of seeds.
   In a month, his ass
   Was all covered with grass,
and his ***** were all covered with weeds.

151

There was a young man of Bombay,
Who thought syphilis just went away,
    And felt that a chancre
    Was merely a canker
Acquired with lascivious play.

152

A lively young lady of Cheltenham
Donned tights to see how she felt in 'em
    But she started to shout:
    "If you don't pull me out
I'm afraid that my **** will melt in 'em."

153

There was a young man from Fleet,
Who minced as he walked down the street.
    He wore shoes of bright red,
    And playfully said:
"I may not be strong, but I'm sweet."

154

There was an old fellow of Maine,
Whose **** was chopped off by a train:
   When his friends said: "How sad!"
   He replied: "It's not bad.
Now I'm rid of my varicose vein."

155

There was a young fellow named Goody,
Who claimed that he wouldn't, but would he?
   If he found himself nude
   With a girl in the mood,
The question's not would he, but could he?

156

An impotent Scot named McDougall
Had to husband his sperm and be frugal.
   He was gathering semen
   To gender a he-man
By *****ing his wife through a bugle.

157

The tarts in the town of Marseilles
Are brunette from the sun every day.
    White wine is their piddle,
    For ten francs they'll diddle—
But their tickets of health, where are they?

158

There was a young pansy named Birch,
Who developed a taste for the Church;
    And monks, priests, and preachers
    And such pious creatures
Were the uplifted ends of his search.

159

I sat next to the Duchess at tea.
It was just as I feared it would be:
    Her rumblings abdominal
    Were simply phenomenal,
And everyone thought it was me.

TWAYL—3

160

A nudist, by name Sextus Peet,
Loved to dance in the snow and the sleet;
    But one chilly December
    He froze every member
And retired to a monastic retreat.

161

I'd rather have fingers than toes,
I'd rather have ears than a nose—
    But a happy erection,
    Brought just to perfection,
Makes me so I just glows.

162

There was a young whore of Shallott,
Who hadn't a hair on her ****.
    She kept it smooth looking
    Not by shaving or plucking,
But by all of the ****ing she got.

163

There was a young fellow named Sweeney,
Whose girl was a terrible meanie.
   The thatch of her snatch
   Had a catch that would latch—
She could only be *****ed by Houdini.

164

There was a young lady of Tottenham,
Who'd no manners, or else had forgotten 'em:
   At tea, at the vicar's,
   She tore off her knickers,
Because, she explained, she felt 'ot in 'em.

165

There was a young lady named Eva,
Who went to a ball as Godiva;
   But a change in the lights
   Showed a tear in her tights,
And a low fellow present yelled: "Beaver!"

166

There was a young man of Rangoon,
Whose farts could be heard on the moon;
    When least you'd expect them,
    They'd burst from his rectum,
With the force of a raging typhoon.

167

There's a charming young lady from Newley,
Who's often been *****ed by yours truly;
    But now—it's appallin'—
    My ***** almost fall in!
I fear that I've ****ed her unduly.

168

A pimply young choirboy named Hugh
Masturbated in the back pew.
    When reproached by the vicar,
    He said: "But, sir, it's quicker
Than when I took lessons from you."

169

There once was a girl from Coblitz,
Who liked to have men bite her tits.
  One good Fletcherizer[16]
  Made her sadder, but wiser,
By chewing them up into bits.

170

There was a young man of Bengal,
Who went to a fancy-dress ball.
  Just for a stunt,
  He went as a ****
And was had by a dog in the hall.

171

There was a young lady of Brid.,[17]
Who wouldn't be done for a quid;
  A dark-eyed Italian
  With ***** like a stallion
Said: "I'll do her for nowt"—*and he did*!

172

There was a young curate of Buckingham,
Who was chided by girls for not ****ing 'em.
    Quoth he: "Though my ****
      Is as hard as a rock,
Your ***** are too slack—put a tuck in 'em!"

173

There was an old lady of Newry,
Whose **** was a *luscus naturae*.
    The *introitus vaginae*
      Was unnaturally tiny,
And the thought of it filled her with fury.

174

While out on a picnic, Magee
Was stung on the ****s by a bee.
    He made oodles of money,
      By exuding clear honey,
Every time he attempted to pee.

175

There was a young girl of Madras,
Who once wore a skirt made of grass;
    But a goat ate a lump
    Of the part round her rump—
The whole of Madras saw her ass.

176

A girl and a boy in a tent
Were thought to be really hell-bent.
    True, he got an erection
    That she viewed with affection—
But that was as far as they went.

177

That man who walked down the Strand,
Holding his ****s in his hand:
    My word! they were thick,
    And massive his *****—
I'm certain his ****ing was grand!

178

A lady was once heard to weep:
"My figure no more can I keep.
   It's my husband's demand
   For a tit in each hand,
And the bastard *will* walk in his sleep."

179

There was a daring young man of Bude,
Who fingered his girl whilst they queued.
   Said a man up in front:
   "I'm sure I smell ****!"
Out loud—just like that—bloody rude!

180

Have you heard about Jasper Lockett?
He was blown down the street by a rocket.
   The force of the blast
   Blew his ***** up his ass,
And his pecker was found in his pocket.[18]

181

A clever young man named McLean
Invented a ****ing machine.
    Concave or convex,
    It would fit either sex,
And was perfectly simple to clean.

182

There was a young girl of Sophia,
Who succumbed to her lover's desire.
    She said : "It's a sin,
    But now that it's in—
Please shove it up higher and higher."

183

A geneticist living in Delft
Secretly played with himself :
    When he had done,
    He labelled it SON,
And filed it away on a shelf.

184

There was a young lady from Dorset,
Who let the boss see her new corset.
   He wrote there a cheque,
   As she lay on her back,
Then took down his pants to endorse it.

185

There was a young student named Chivy,
Who, whenever he went to the privy,
   First solaced his mind,
   Then wiped his behind,
With some well-chosen pages of Livy.

186

There was a young lady of Ealing,
Who professed to lack sexual feeling—
   But a cynic named Boris
   Just touched her clitoris,
And she had to be scraped off the ceiling.

187

A randy young fellow called Lunt
Told his friend he was out on the hunt.
    Said the friend: "Have a tot."
    He replied: "Oh, you clot,
It's not whisky I'm hunting, it's ****."

188

A pert miss, for a fault of decorum,
Was tanned by her father at Shoreham.
    It quite painfully hurt
    When he'd pulled up her skirt,
Her fault was she just never wore 'em.

189

A singer who lived in Lahore
Got his ****s caught up in a door.
    Now his *mezzavoce*
    Is all *sotto voce*
Though he was a loud *basso* before.

190

There was a young lady of Eton,
Whose figure had plenty of meat on.
   She said : "Marry me, Jim,
    And you'll find that my ****
Is a nice place to warm your cold feet on."

191

A jolly old Bishop of Birmingham,
He rogered three maids while confirming 'em.
   As they knelt seeking God,
    He excited his rod,
And pumped his episcopal sperm in 'em.

192

Sprightly Miss Coles of Coleshill
Sat on the hole of a mole's hill.
   The resident mole
    Stuck his nose up the hole :
Miss Coles is all right—but Mole's ill !

193

I dined with Lord Hughie Fitz-Bluing,
Who said: "Do you squirm when you're
      *****ing?"
  I replied: "Simple *****ing
  Without any wagging
Is only for *****ing canoeing."

194

There was a young lady from Nance,
Who performed a sexual dance.
    Forty-five ****ed her,
    Besides the conductor,
And the drummer came off in his pants.

195

There was an old man of Calcutta,
Who peeped through a hole in a shutter.
    All he could see
    Was the prostitute's knee
And the **** of the man who was up 'er.

196

There was a young man of Warwick,
Who had reason for feeling euphoric;
    For he could by election
    Have triune erection—
Ionic, Corinthian, Doric.

197

There was a young lady of Kew,
Who said as the Bishop withdrew:
    "The dear Vicar is quicker
    And slicker and thicker
And three inches longer than you."

198

An impressionable curate from Cambs
Said: "These mini-skirt girls are such lambs;
    But my duties I'm lax in,
    And my vows get such cracks in,
When from my knees I see all their young hams."

199

I could hear the dull buzz of the bee
As he sunk his grub hooks into me.
 Her ass it was fine,
 But you should have seen mine,
In the shade of the old apple tree.

200

An innocent girl said: "Lumme, Mum!
I fear I'll soon be a mummy, Mum.
 I know it was fun
When we done what we done,
But he lied when he called it a dummy run!"

201

There was a nutty young fellow named Smart,
Who rogered his maid for a start;
 Then with a whoopee of glee
 He started to pee
All over his mum's cherry tart.

202

There was a young lady of Ealing,
Said to her beau : "I've a feeling
  My little brown jug
  Has need of a plug!"—
And straightaway started to peeling.

203

There was a young monk of Siberia,
Who of *****ing grew wearier and wearier :
  Till at last, with a yell,
  He burst from his cell,
And ******ed the Father Superior.

204

A maiden from Ballyjamesduff
Had a pussy as large as a muff.
  It had room for both hands
  And some intimate glands
And was soft as a little duck's fluff.

205

There was a young man from Cape Cod,
Who put his own mother in pod.
   His name? It was Tucker,
   The dirty young ****er,
The Bugger! The Bastard! The Sod!

206

To his bride said the lynx-eyed detective,
"Can it be that my eyesight's defective?
   Has the east tit the least bit
   The best of the west tit—
Or is it the faulty perspective?"

207

There was a young man of Calcutta,
Who tried to write "****" on a shutter.
   He had got to "c-u-"
   When a pious Hindu
Kicked him ass over face in the gutter.

208

A mother of ten, who was carrying,
Said: "Your father the police are still harrying.
   He's a liar and thief
   And drinks past belief,
To be honest, I'm glad I didn't marry him."

209

There was a young priest named Delaney,
Who said to the girls: "*Nota bene*:
   I've seen how you swish up
   Your skirts at the bishop
Whenever the weather is rainy."[19]

210

Van Gogh found a whore who would lay,
And accept a small painting as pay.
   "*Vive l'Art!*" cried Van Gogh.
   "But it's too bloody slow—
I wish I could paint ten a day."

211

There was a young couple of Aberystwyth,
Who coupled the things that they kissed with;
    But as they grew older,
    They soon became bolder,
And coupled the things that they pissed with.

212

There was a young Royal Marine,
Who tried to fart "God Save the Queen".
    When he reached the soprano,
    Out came the guano,
And his breeches weren't fit to be seen.

213

There was a young gaucho named Bruno,
Who said: "****ing is one thing I do know.
    A woman is fine
    And a sheep is divine,
But a llama is *numero uno*."

214

There was a young lady of Cheadle,
Who sat down in church on a needle :
   Though deeply embedded,
   'Twas luckily threaded,
And she had it pulled out by the beadle.

215

There was a young man of Australia,
Who went on a wild bacchanalia.
   He ******ed a frog,
   Two mice and a dog—
And a bishop in fullest regalia.

216

All loyal Britons will applaud
A Britain-backing bawd name of Maud ;
   For she went to the States,
   Where she charged double rates,
Thus earning many dollars abroad.

217

There once was a man from Geneva,
Who ******ed a black bitch retriever.
   The result was a sow,
   Two horses, a cow,
Three llamas and a London coal-heaver.

218

There was a young lady from Leicester,
Who said to the man who undressed her:
   "If you want a good grind,
   Best go in from behind,
As the front is beginning to fester."

219

In a meadow a man named Llewellyn
Had a dream he was bundling with Helen.
   When he awoke he discovered
   A bull had him covered
With ******** as big as a melon.

220

A tarty young lady from Ealing
Pinned Gauguin reproductions on her ceiling.
   Coupling passion for art
   With her work as a tart,
She achieved quite a sensitive feeling.

221

The honeymoon couple begun,
But the bed springs were so overstrung,
   That the rhythm soon harassed
   Their duet and embarrassed—
So they left the finale unsung.

222

There was a young lady from Spain,
Who liked a bit now and again.
   Not now and again—
   But NOW and again,
And again, and again, and AGAIN!

223

A nasty young man from Belgrave
Kept a dead whore in a cave,
    Saying: "I must admit,
    I'm a bit of a ****,
But just think of the money I save!"

224

There was a young lady from Rider,
Who went to bed with a tiger.
    The result of the ****
    Was a four-legged duck,
An ant, and a castrated spider.

225

Remember that couple of Aberystwyth
Who coupled the things that they pissed with?
    When she sat on his lap
    They both had the clap,
And cursed with the things that they kissed with.

226

There was a young fellow named Paul,
Who was able to bounce either ****.
   He could stretch them and snap them,
   And juggle and clap them,
Which earned him the plaudits of all.

227

There was a young woman of Moyence,
Who bade Adolf Hitler defiance.
   She'd lurk in dark halls
   And nip at his ****s
With a patent-applied-for appliance.

228

There was a young fellow called Clunk
With a donk like an elephant's trunk:
   When it stiffened and rose,
   It reached up to his nose,
And when tossed it gave gallons of *****.

229

There was a pure lady of Thame,
Who resolved to live free from blame
   She wore four pairs of drawers,
   And of petticoats, scores:
She was ****ed in the end just the same.

230

Two schoolboys at play on the grass
Found it hard to make time quickly pass.
   So being good sports,
   They discarded their shorts,
And each bounced up and down on his ass.

231

A pretty young schoolgirl asked: "What
Should I do with my elegant ****?
   When it's wet and it's hot
   And it's itching a lot
Tell me please—should I wipe it or not?"

232

A spunky young schoolboy named Ted
Used to toss every night while in bed.
    Said his mother: "My lad,
    That's exceedingly bad—
From now on you'll **** me instead."

233

There was a young lady of Exeter,
So fair that all men craned their necks at her;
    But one more depraved
    Than the rest boldly waved
The distinguishing mark of his sex at her.

234

There was a young man who said: "Who
Will show me the way to a loo?
    For I must have a piss;
    In addition to this,
I'm just itching to masturbate too."

235

There was a young girl from Uttoxeter,
And all the young men waved their ***** at her;
    But from one of these ****s
    She contracted the pox:
Now she's poxed all the ****s in Uttoxeter.[21]

236

A vice both obscene and unsavoury
Held a Master of Balliol in slavery.
    With bloodcurdling howls
    He deflowered young owls
That he kept in an underground aviary.[22]

237

There was a young lady named Sally,
Who was dancing one night in the ballet.
    There were roars of applause
    When down fell her drawers—
For the hair on her head didn't tally.

238

There was a young man from Wood's Hole,
Who had an affair with a mole.
   Though a bit of a nancy,
   He did like to fancy,
Himself in a dominant role.

239

There was a young girl named Bianca,
Who retired while the ship was at anchor;
   But awoke, with dismay,
   When she heard the mate say:
"We must pull up the top sheet and spank her."

240

His Lordship the Bishop of Dude,
He played with a blonde in the nude;
   But she said: "Oh, my Lord,
   With plain ****ing I'm bored.
Can't we do something really lewd?"

241

A keeper in Hamburg's great zoo
Tried to roger a girl kangaroo ;
   But she zipped up her pouch
   Which made him cry : "Ouch !
   You've got a half ***** in you ! "

242

There was a young man of Belgravia,
Who cared neither for God nor for Saviour.
   He walked down the Strand
   With his ****s in his hand,
And was had up for indecent behaviour.[28]

243

Sir Reginald Beaumondsey, Bart.,
Went to a masked ball as a fart.
   He had painted his face
   Like a more private place—
His voice made the dowagers start.

244

There was a young lady at court,
Who said to the King, with a snort:
    "Was it humour, or shyness
    That prompted Your Highness
To put Spanish Fly in my port?"

245

A musical young man named Canute
Was dismayed by the warts on his ****.
    He put acid on these
    And now, when he pees,
He can tootle his **** like a flute.

246

There was young lady of Ghat,
Who never could sit but she ****.
    Oh, the seat of her drawers
    Was a chamber of horrors—
And think how they felt when she sat.

247

A lively young scholar of King's
Had no use for pretty young things;
    But the height of his joy
    Was a fat-bottomed boy
With an **** like a jelly on springs.

248

There was a young lady from China,
Who mistook for her mouth her vagina.
    Her clitoris huge
    She covered with rouge,
And lipsticked her labia minor.

249

There was an old fellow from Kent,
Whose ***** was all battered and bent.
    While having a ****
    He once ran amok,
And instead of his coming, he went.

250

There was a young lady named Duff
With a lovely luxuriant muff.
   In his haste to get in her,
   One avid beginner
Lost both of his ****s in the rough.

251

A ballistical student named Raffity
Went down to a gentlemen's laffity.
   When the walls met his sight,
   He said : "Newton was right—
This must be the centre of graffiti."

252

There was a young girl called Hicks
Who delighted to play with men's *****s,
   Which she would embellish
   With evident relish,
And make them stand up and do tricks.

253

There was a young fellow of Rye Hill,
Who, wanting to crap, climbed a high hill.
    Upon his descent,
    When asked how it went,
He said: *"Vox et praetoria nihil."*

254

A lady by passion deluded
Found an African drunk and denuded;
    And—fit as a fiddle,
    And hot for a diddle—
She tied splints to his ***** and *****ed it.

255

There was a young girl of Penzance,
Who went to a Birth Control dance,
    Complete with accessories,
    French letters and pessaries,
And then had to dance with a nance.

256

This new cinematic emporium
Is not a *censori censorium,*
   But a highly effectual,
   Heterosexual,
Mutual *masturbatorium.*

257

There was a young sailor named Bates,
Who did a fandango on skates;
   But fell on his cutlass,
   Which rendered his nutless,
And just about useless on dates.

258

A useless young fellow of Kent
Had his wife **** the landlord for rent.
   But as she grew older
   The landlord grew colder,
And now they live out in a tent.

259

An obliging young barmaid called Belle
Kept a file of her best clientele.
   By recording their tastes
   Right up to their waists,
She gave value for money as well.

260

Impotent Seamus O'Shea,
When his ***** wouldn't rise for a lay:
   "Please seize it, and squeeze it,
   And tease it, and please it—
For Rome wasn't built in a day."

261

An ignorant maiden named Sue-Pidd
Did something exceedingly stupid:
   When her lover had spent,
   She douched with cement,
And gave birth to a statue of Cupid.

262

A daring young curate from Crewe
Was addressed by a wench: "How d'ye do?"
   He said: "This is nice!"
   Unzipped in a trice,
And showed her a thing and a two.

263

There was a young girl whose propriety
Caused all her young swains great anxiety:
   For in spite of their urgin'
   She resolved to stay virgin—
Which at least gives these verses variety!

264

A learned professor from Buckingham
Wrote a treatise on ****s and on sucking 'em;
   But later his work
   Was eclipsed by a Turk
Whose subject was ****-holes and ****ing 'em.

265

There was a young housewife of Rhyl,
Who decided to try out the Pill;
    But she took the wrong one—
    Yeastex—now the bun
In the oven is rising at will.

266

There was a young laundress of Glamas,
Who invented high amorous dramas
    From the spots she espied
    Dried and hardened inside
The pants of the parson's pyjamas.

267

The witch-doctor felt quite bemused,
For the young female patient enthused
    On his unctions and potions,
    His functions and motions,
And whichever witchcraft he had used.

268

There was an old gent of Baroda,
Who wouldn't pay a girl what he owed her.
    Said she : "What a sod.
    Wants **** on the nod."
So she spat in his whisky and soda.

269

There was a young lady from Spain,
Whose face was exceedingly plain ;
    But her **** had a pucker
    That made the men **** her
Again, and again, and again.

270

There was a young man whose desire
Was to raise up some primeval fire.
    The resulting conflagration
    Caused quite a sensation,
For he laid every girl in the shire.

271

The team of Bert and Louise
Do an act in the nude on their knees.
   They crawl down the aisle
   While ****ing dog style,
While the orchestra sweetly plays "Trees".

272

There was a young fellow named Rex,
Who had a small organ of sex.
   When charged with exposure,
   He said, with composure,
"De minibus non caput lex."

273

The incumbent Vicar of Bray
Kept his wife in the family way.;
   Till she grew more alert,
   Bought a vaginal squirt,
And quipped to her spouse: "Let us spray!"

274

There was a young lady named Roose,
Whose favourite thrill was a goose;
    Just the sight of a thumb
    Caused her anus to hum
And her bowels got excited—and loose.[24]

275

A volcanic eruption in Java
Led the Baron de Fritzin Palaver.
    In that moment sublime,
    To bequeath for all time
The imprint of his ****s in the lava.

276

If you're speaking of actions immoral,
Then how about giving the laurel
    To doughty young Esther
    No three men could best her—
One fore, one aft, and one oral.

277

A mathematician named Hall
Had a hexahedronical ball.
 The cube of its weight
 Times his pecker, plus eight,
Was four-fifths of five-eighths of ****-all.

278

An old couple just at Shrovetide
Were having a piece—when he died.
 The wife for a week
 Sat tight on his peak,
And bounced up and down as she cried.

279

There was a young man of St. James',
Who went in for the jolliest games.
 He set fire to the rim
 Of his grandmother's ****,
Then roared as she pissed through the flames.

280

A randy hildalgo of Spain
****ed a girl-friend of his in the train;
   On the floor by the door,
   Not once and no more,
But again and again and AGAIN.

281

There was an old abbess quite shocked
To find nuns where the candles were locked.
   Said the abbess: "You nuns
   Should behave just like guns
And never go off till you're cocked."

282

There was a young man from Australia,
Who painted his ass like a dahlia.
   The drawing was fine,
   The colour divine:
The scent—Ah! There was the failure.

283

There was an old chap from the Cape,
Who ******ed a Barbary ape.
   The ape said : "You fool !
   Your ugly square ****
Has ******ed my **** out of shape."

284

There was a young nun from Siberia,
Who was endowed with a virgin exterior—
   Till a virile young monk
   Leapt into her bunk ;
And now she's the Mother Superior.

285

There was a young man of Devizes,
Whose ****s were of different sizes.
   One was so small
   It was no use at all—
But the other won twenty "First Prizes".

286

A young fellow, about to be wed,
Took a course of six lessons on "Bed".
   When shown how to do it,
   He said : "There's nowt to it—
I could do that all night on my head."

287

There was a young whore of Crewe,
Who filled her vagina with glue.
   Said she with a grin :
   "If they pay to get in,
They'll pay to get out of it too."

288

That same young man of Devizes,
Whose **** won numerous prizes :
   His ****, when at ease,
   Hung down to his knees—
Oh, what must it be when it rises !

289

A hapless young girl from Devon,
Was raped in the garden by seven
   High Anglican Priests—
   Lascivious beasts!—
Of such is the Kingdom of Heaven!

290

The intestines of Dante Rossetti[25]
Were exceedingly fragile and petty:
   All he could eat
   Was finely chopped meat,
And all he could **** was spaghetti

291

There was an old Bey of Calcutta,
Who greased up his ass-hole with butter.
   Instead of the roar
   Which came there before,
Came a soft, oleaginous mutter.

292

There was a young lady of Trent,
Who said that she knew what it mean
   When men asked her to dine,
   Private room, lots of wine:
She knew, oh she knew!—but she went!

293

An entrepreneur from Australia
Once painted his bum like a dahlia.
   Threepence a smell
   Went very well,
But sixpence a lick was a failure.

294

When asked by the Duchess at tea,
If an egg-plant I ever did see?
   I said: "Yes", rather bored;
   She said: "Sir, you've explored
Up a hen's **** much further than me."

295

Again : that young man of Devizes,
Odd winner of numerous prizes :
   His ****, when at ease,
   Hangs down to his knees,
And tickles his chin when it rises.

296

There was a pious young priest,
Who lived almost wholly on yeast.
   He said : "It is plain
   We must all rise again
So it's fun to get started at least."

297

There was a young girl of Penzance,
Who boarded a bus in a trance.
   The passengers ****ed her,
   Also the conductor,
While the driver shot off in his pants.

298

There was a young man of Tibet,
And this is the strangest one yet—
    His ***** was so long,
    And so pointed and strong,
He could ****er six Turks *en brochette*.

299

There was a young lady named Alice,[26]
Who peed in the Vatican Palace.
    It wasn't her need
    Which fostered the deed,
But deliberate Protestant malice.

300

There was a young fellow called Horton,
Who had an exceedingly short 'un.
    He made good the loss
    With the ****s of a horse
And a stroke like a "500" c.c. Norton.

301

When a charmer in strapless attire
Found her breasts working higher and higher,
   A guest, with great feeling,
   Exclaimed: "How appealing!
Do you mind if I piss in the fire?"

302

There was a bold lad of Kildare,
Who was ****ing a girl on the stair:
   At the eighty-third stroke
   The banister broke,
And his weapon shot off in the air

303

A lady of virginal humours
Would only be *****ed through her bloomers.
   But one fatal day
   The bloomers gave way—
Which fixed her for future consumers.

304

There was a young man of Pitlochry,
Whose morals were simply a mock'ry.
   For under his bed
   He'd a woman, instead
Of the usual item of crock'ry.

305

There was a young lady of Rhyll,
In an omnibus said she felt ill,
   The randy conductor
   Sprang up and ****ed her—
Which did her more good than a pill.

306

An explorer returned from Australia
Reported lost paraphernalia:
   A Zeiss microscope,
   And his personal hope,
Which had vanished with his genitalia.

307

Said a strange young man of Blackheath:
"I ought not to wear my best sheath.
   But what can I do?
   I only have two,
And the other has a leak underneath."

308

An adroit young nurse of Japan
Lifts men by their *****s to the pan:
   A trick of jujitsu
   And either it ****s you
Or makes you feel more of a man.

309

An ingenious musician called Boris
Used to fondle a girl in his Morris.
   From the beat on her tits
   He'd score Top Twenty Hits,
With counterpoint from her clitoris.

310

There was a young woman called Gloria,
Who was had by Sir Hotpoint Effloria;
   Then by ten men,
   Sir Hotpoint again,
And the band at the Waldorf Astoria.

311

A cardinal living in Rome
Had a Renaissance bath in his home.
   He could gaze at his nudes
   As he worked up his moods
In emulsions of ***** and foam.

312

A homely old spinster of France,
At whom all the men looked askance,
   Threw her skirt overhead
   And then jumped into bed,
Saying: "Now I've at least half a chance!"

313

There was a young man from Bengal
Who went to a fancy-dress ball.
    He went as a tree,
    Having failed to foresee
Being peed on by dogs, cats, and all.

314

Said a smart young hiker named Glad,
When she'd picked up a likely lad:
    "We can't satisfy Adam
    On this cold tarmacadam,
So let's go back home to my pad."

315

A swami once took Spanish Fly
And ran clean amok in Delhi,
    Where he jumped in the Ganges
    And used his phalanges
To comfort the ****s swimming by.

316

A lady schoolteacher of Devizes
Was had up at the local assizes,
    For teaching young boys
    Matrimonial joys,
And giving French letters as prizes.

317

There was a young man from Glenchasm,
Who had a tremendous orgasm:
    In the midst of his thralls
    He burst both his ****s
And covered an acre with plasm.

318

There was a young lady of Skye
With a shape like a capital "I".
    She said: "It's too bad,
    But then I can pad."
Which just shows how figures can lie.

319

There once was a sailor from Wales,
An expert at pissing in gales.
   He could piss in a jar
   From the top-gallant spar,
Without even wetting the sails.

320

There was a young girl of Samoa,
Who determined that no man should know her.
   A young fellow tried,
   But she wriggled aside,
And spilled all his spermatozoa.

321

There was a young fellow named Jim,[27]
Who took a girl out for a swim;
   But too lazy to rape her,
   He made darts of brown paper,
Which he languidly tossed at her ****.

322

She slept with a man from the Rand,
Whose ***** could contract or expand.
　　He could get through a midge,
　　Or the arch of a bridge,
And between them the going was grand.

323

There was a young man who said: "Why
Can't I ****er myself if I try?
　　If I put my mind to it,
　　I'm sure I can do it—
You never can tell till you try."

324

There was a young lady named Hilda,
Who went for a walk with a builder.
　　He knew that he could—
　　He should, and he would—
He did—and goddam near killed her!

325

There was an old man of Dundee,
Who came home as drunk as could be.
 He wound up the clock
 With the end of his ****,
And ******ed his wife with the key.[28]

326

A lady composer of Trim
Possessed a remarkable ****.
 It sang *arioso*
 In tones *curioso*,
And even the occasional hymn.

327

A frustrated young man from Belgrave,[29]
Came across a dead whore in a cave.
 Now, perhaps t'was bad luck
 To have a cold ****,
But he thought of the money he'd save.

328

A certain old harpy from Umsk,
Who was wholly unable to cumsk,
  Would ecstatically shout
  When a samovar spout
Was shoved up her Muscovite rumpsk.[30]

329

A young necrophiliac called Tasker
Had a love life that was a disaster.
  As his blushes he hid,
  He said: "I lift up the lid
But can't pluck up the courage to ask her."

330

There was a young lady of Harrow,
Who complained that her **** was too narrow;
  For time without number
  She could use a cucumber,
But could not accomplish a marrow.

331

There once was a Bishop of Chichester,
Who took a young girl into a nichester.
    Her voluptuous figure,
    Her zest and her vigour,
Made a lump in the Bishop's britches stir.

332

There was a young lady of Spain,
Who went and undressed in the train;
    But a saucy young porter
    Saw more than he oughter
And plugged her again and again.

333

A young man, quite free with his dong,
Said the thing could be had for a song.
    Such response did he get
    That he rented the Met
And held auditions all day long.

334

There was an old girl of Nantucket,
Who went down to hell in a bucket;
   And the last words she spoke,
   Before the rope broke,
Were "Assholes, you ****ers, and suck it!"

335

There was a young girl from Peru,
Who was lost for a want of a *****;
   She tried a broom-handle,
   Both ends of a candle,
But threw them away for a Jew.

336

There was an old man of Blackheath,
What sat on his set of false teeth.
   Said he, with a start:
   "Oh, Lord, bless my heart!
I fear I'm desexed underneath."

337

There was a young girl, name of Rose,
Who'd occasionally straddle a hose,
    And parade about, squirting
    And spouting and spurting,
Pretending she pissed like her beaux.

338

A medieval recluse named Sissions
Was alarmed by his nightly emissions.
    His cell-mate, a sod,
    Said: "Leave it to God,"
And taught him some nifty positions.

339

On the breasts of a typist called Brenda
Were inscribed all kinds of agenda;
    And first names of her bosses,
    Their profits and losses,
Were tattooed on her fulsome pudenda.

340

There was a young man with a hernia,
Who said to his surgeon: "God dernya!
   When carving my middle,
   Be sure you don't fiddle
With matters that don't concernya."[31]

341

There was a young lady named May,
Who strolled in the park one fine day.
   She met there a man
   Who ****ed her and ran—
Now she goes to the park every day.

342

While Titian was mixing rose-madder,
His model posed nude on a ladder.
   Her position, to Titian,
   Suggested coition,
So he climbed up the ladder and 'ad 'er.

343

There was a young fellow named Paul,
Whose act always brought down the hall:
    For his finishing trick
    Was to stand on his *****
And wheel out of the hall on one ****.

344

'Twas a fearful and wonderful sight
And the ladies all screamed with delight;
    But the men were less zealous,
    For it made them all jealous,
And they said that it wasn't polite.

345

But that night each one tried it and failed,
While their wives looked on helpless and wailed:
    For either they'd teeter
    And fall off their *****,
Or they'd find themselves getting derailed.

346

So Paul was the toast of the town,
With nothing too good for the clown;
    And the wives came flocking
    To witness his ****ing,
While their husbands deplored his renown.

347

A neurotic virgin named Flynn
Shouted before she gave in:
    "It isn't the deed
    Or the fear of the seed,
But that big worm that's shedding its skin!"

348

An uxorious fellow from Fife
Found a stranger in bed with his wife.
    He cried: "Ah! wanton creature!
    Perhaps this will teach yer!"
And he removed the man's ****s with a knife.

349

There was a young lady named Flynn,
Who considered fornication a sin;
   But when she was tight
   It seemed quite all right—
So she kept filling up with gin.

350

There was an old Scot of Glencoo,
Who could always find something to do.
   When it bored him (you know?),
   To **** to and fro,
He would change and **** fro and to.

351

There was an old lady of Leicester,
And no man had ever possessed her.
   But all day she'd wriggle
   And giggle and giggle
As though seven devils possessed her.

352

A godly young novice in Deal,
Said: "Although sex isn't real,
   When Sister Sabina
   Dilates my vagina
I quite like what I fancy I feel."[32]

353

There was a young lady of Louth,
Who returned from a trip to the South.
   He mother said: "Nelly,
   There's more in your belly,
Than ever went in by your mouth."

354

There was a young man of Madras,
Who made a French letter of brass.
   When to bed he retired
   The darn thing back-fired
And blew off the back of his ass.

355

There was a young lady of Tahaiti,
Whom the neighbours decided was flahiti;
   For if Monday was fine,
    You could see, on the line,
A rather diaphanous nahiti.

356

There was a young fellow named Charteris,
Who put his hand where his lady's garter is.
   She said: "I don't mind
    But up higher you'll find
The place where my ****er and farter is."

357

There was a young lady of Keighley,
Whose principal charm in her teeth lay;
   When they fell on her plate,
    She called out: "I hate
Mishaps of this kind—they are beathly."

358

The Marquesa de Excusador[33]
Used to pee on the drawing-room floor;
   For the can was so cold,
   And when one grows old
To be much alone is a bore.

359

Said an elderly whore called Arlene:
"I prefer a young lad of eighteen.
   There's more cream in his larder
   And his ***** gets harder,
And he ****s in a manner obscene."

360

There was a young fellow from Churt,
Who shoved his hand up a girl's skirt.
   She liked it so much,
   He then let her touch
The thing he'd got under his shirt.

361

Three innocent ladies of Grimsby
Said: "What use can our three ****s be?
    The hole in the middle
    Is so we can piddle,
But for what can the hair round the rims be?"

362

An elderly pervert in Nice,
Who was long past wanting a piece,
    Would jack-off his hogs,
    His cows and his dogs,
Till his parrot called in the police.

363

A pretty young lady called Damson
Was raped in the back of a hansom:
    When she hollered for more
    A voice gasped from the floor:
"The name, Miss, is Hanson, not Samson!"

364

A young man with passions very gingery
Tore a hole in his sister's best lingerie.
   He goosed her behind
   And made up his mind
To add incest to insult and injury.

365

An entrancing young lady from Whiston
Thought her bum an odd place to be kissed on.
   So she turned on her back,
   Showed her lover her *****,
And demanded: "Now work like a piston!"

366

There was a young man named Hughes,
Who swore off all kinds of booze.
   He said: 'When I'm muddled
   My senses get fuddled,
And I pass up too many *****s."

367

An eccentric young lady of Herm
Tied bows on the tail of a sperm.
 Said she: "You look festive,
 But don't become restive,
You'll wriggle 'em off if you squirm."

368

There was a young sailor from Brighton,
Who said to his girl: "You've a tight 'un."
 She replied: "Pon my soul!
 You're in the wrong hole!
But there's plenty of room in the right 'un!"

369

There once was a young lady of Cheam
Whose desire for a man was extreme:
 With her thighs open wide,
 She said: Oh! come inside"—
But alas! it was only a dream.

370

Il y avait plombier, Dubois,[34]
Qui plombait sa femme dans le Bois.
    Dit-elle : "Arretez !
    J'entende quelqu'un venait."
Dit le plombier, en plombant : "C'est moi."

371

A thrifty young lady of Shoreham
Made brown-paper knickers and woreham.
    She looked nice and neat
    Till she bent in the street
To pick up a pin—then she toreham.

372

There was a young fellow from Sparta,
A truly mellifluous farter.
    On the strength of one bean,
    He'd fart "God Save the Queen"
And Beethoven's "Moonlight Sonata".

373

There was a young girl from Madrid,
Who swore that she'd never be rid;
   Till she met an Italian,
   With ****s like a stallion,
Who swore that he would—and he did!

374

There was an old man of Peru,
Who found he had nothing to do.
   So he sat on the stairs
   And counted crotch hairs—
"Eight thousand, four hundred, and two."

375

There was an old lady who lay
With her legs wide apart in the hay.
   Then, calling the ploughman,
   She said: "Do it now, man!
Don't wait till your hair's turning grey!"

376

There was a young man of Lahore,
Whose ***** was one inch and no more.
   It was all right for key-holes
    And little girl's pee-holes,
But not worth a damn with a whore.

377

An inquisitive maid from Peru
Used to wonder what young couples do ;
   So she spied through a keyhole
    Where she saw a girl's pee-hole
Being rammed, and said : "I'd like some too."

378

There was a young monk of Kilkyre,
Who was smitten by carnal desire.
   The immediate cause
    Was the abbess's drawers
She had hung up to dry by the fire.

379

There is a young girl of Kilkenny,
Who is troubled by suitors so many,
    That the saucy young elf
    Means to raffle herself,
And the tickets are two for a penny.

380

A sailor ashore in Peru
Said: "Signora, quanto por la screw?"
    "For only one peso,
    I will, if you say so,
Be ******ed and nibble it too."

381

There was a young lady of Wilts,
Who walked to the Highlands on stilts.
    When folk said: "Oh, how shocking
    To show so much stocking!"
She answered: "Well, how about kilts?"

382

There was a young fellow of Harrow,
Whose **** was the size of a marrow.
   He said to a tart:
   "How's this for a start?
I carry my ****s in a barrow."

383

A young lady with hair à la Titian
Went one day to consult a physician.
   When she stripped, he declared:
   "That's the first golden-haired
Pubis I've seen—howzabout some coition?"

384

When Abelard near Notre Dame
Had taught fair Heloise the game,
   Her uncle—the wag—
   Cut off Peter's bag,
And his lectures were never the same.

385

There was a young man of Nantucket,
Whose ***** was so long he could suck it.
   Said he, with a grin,
   As he wiped clean his chin:
"If my ear was a **** I could **** it."

386

A young lady from Tottenham Court Road
Used to dress in an unusual mode:
   Both her tits she left bare,
   And her bright pubic hair
Through her transparent skirt always showed.

387

Ethnologists up with the Sioux
Wired home for two punts, one canoe.
   The answer, next day,
   Said: GIRLS ON THE WAY
BUT WHAT THE HELL'S A PANOE?"

388

"It's been such a wonderful day,"
Sighed Lady M'Gimpsie McKay.
   "Five cherry tarts,
   At least forty farts,
Three ****s and a bloody fine lay."

389

There's a wealthy young man from Bagdad,
Whose morals are terribly bad.
   He keeps seven Circassians
   As a vent for his passions—
In fact he's a hell of a lad.

390

There was an old lady of Lee,
Who scrambled up into a tree.
   When they got there
   Her asshole was bare,
And so was her * * * *.

391

A suspicious old husband from Funtua
To his wife said: "How bulky in front you are.
   You have not been imprudent
   I should hope, with some student?"
She replied: "Really, dear, how blunt you are!"

392

There was a young lady called Randell,
Who caused such a terrible scandal,
   By coming out bare
   On the main village square
And making improper use of a candle.

393

Withdrawal, according to Freud,
Is a very good thing to avoid.
   If practised each day,
   One's ****s will decay
To the size of a small adenoid.

394

"Freud's opinion," said Dr. Stekel,
"Isn't worth a confederate shekel.
    Withdrawal is fun—
    But beware lest the sun
Should cause the withdrawn parts to freckle."

395

A girl met a boy so moronic
He thought love should be quite platonic.
    She explained, just to tease,
    About the birds and the bees—
But she shrieked with voice highly sonic.

396

A bobby of Clapham Junction,
Whose organ had long ceased to function,
    Deceived his good wife
    For the rest of her life
With the help of his constable's truncheon.

397

Es giebt ein Arbeiter von Tinz,
Er schlaft mit ein Madel von Linz.
   Sie sagt: "Haltsein' plummen,
   Ich hore mann kommen."
"Jacht, jacht," sagt der Plummer, "ich binz."

398

There was a gay countess of Bray,
And you may think it odd when I say
   That in spite of high station,
   Rank and education,
She always spelt **** with a K.

399

There once was a girl named McGoffin,
Who was diddled amazingly often.
   She was rogered by scores
   Who'd been turned down by whores,
And was finally screwed in a coffin.

400

A pigmy with heedless affront
Called out in Hyde Park: "I want ****!"
    He looked all around,
    But not one could be found—
So he just rhododendron—the runt!

401

There was a young lady of Clewer,
Who was riding a bike and it threw her.
    A man saw her there
    With her legs in the air,
And seized the occasion to ***** her.

402

There was a short-kilted North Briton,
Who promiscuously sat on a kitten;
    But the kitten had claws—
    The immediate cause
Of that North Briton's abrupt circumcision.

403

A skinny old maid of Verdun
Wed a short-peckered son-of-a-gun.
   She said: "I don't care
   If there isn't much there.
God knows it is better than none."

404

A lascivious maid from Ardglass,
Reclined with a monk on the grass.
   She lifted his frock
   And tickled his ****
Till it foamed like a bottle of Bass.

405

A prudish blue-stocking in Florence
Wrote anti-sex pamphlets in torrents,
   Till a Spanish grandee
   Got her off with his knee—
And she burned all her works with abhorrence.

406

There once was a young man from Walsall,
Who, poor fellow, had only one ****;
   But this fact, when in bed,
   So the girls always said,
Didn't lessen his vigour at all.

407

A viscious old whore from Albania
Hated men with a terrible mania.
   With a twitch and a squirm,
   She'd hold back your sperm,
And then roll on your face and disdain ya.[35]

408

There was an old vicar of Hestion,
Who'd erect at the slightest suggestion;
   But so small was his ****,
   He could scarce ***** a spool,
And a **** was quite out of the question.

409

An eccentric young virgin from Dallas
Was invited to Westminster Palace.
  When they showed her Black Rod,
  She said: "Gee, boys, that's odd;
I'd have thought it meant a black phallus."

410

There was a young fellow from Oudh,
Whose mind was excessively lewd.
  He asserted: "All women
  Seen dancin' or swimmin'
Would rather be home getting *****ed."

411

There was a shy boy named Dan,
Who tickled his girl with a fan.
  She started to flirt
  So he lifted her skirt
And gave her a **** like a man.

412

Pity the spermatozoa!
His life leads him lower and lower.
    With fire in his belly,
    He swims through the jelly,
But seldom increases the scoah.

413

There once was an eager young physician,[36]
Who linked practice with vast erudition;
    He thought it a crime
    To waste any time,
So he read while engaged in coition.

NOTES

[1] (7) For reasons discussed in the foreword, it is hardly surprising that officers of the Church should feature often in limericks, behaving uncharacteristically either verbally or in deed, and succumbing to those lusts of the flesh they normally preach against. During the competition craze period the Church provided the largest proportion of limerick enthusiasts among the professions. And they showed an admirable predilection for poking fun at themselves. (A vicar, who shall be nameless, provided a number of limericks for this volume.)

[2] (16) One of the many limericks still commonly heard in Britain, yet included in the first anthology of ribald limericks the writer has been able to trace: *Lady Cythera's Hymnal* or *Flakes from the Foreskin,* London, 1870.

[3] (18) A very old limerick and perhaps the best known in Britain. There are several variantts. Can be Lea or Leigh.

[4] (34) This famous "limersick" has been attributed to Alfred Lord Tennyson. Certainly, it has a vigour worthy of a great poet. Many celebrated poets and writers were said to have composed limericks for private entertainment, including Swinburne, Dante Gabriel Rossetti, Tennyson, Ruskin, Rudyard Kipling and James Joyce.

[5] (37) Justly considered a splendid limerick. The tone is conversational; there is real style; the short words trot along as regularly as a high-stepping pony; a fascinating incident in high society described most effectively with the minimum of words, and with a

line to spare for an apt comment.

[6] (40) A limerick, of which there are a number, in which the use of an affected "upper class" English pronunciation is necessary for correct rhyming—"parkahs", "starkahs".

[7] (60) First published 1879, in London, in a magazine called *The Pearl* (1879/80). The limericks appeared under the heading "Nursery Rhymes". A successor from the same publisher, Cameron, was called *The Cremorne,* and its first issue of August 1882 was craftily dated January 1851.

[8] (78) Similar natural abilities are attributed to a young girl from La Plata.

[9] (81) The philosophical limerick, of which the most celebrated is :

> There was a young man who said : "Damn !
> It is borne upon me that I am
> But a being that moves
> In predestinate grooves—
> I'm not even a bus, I'm a tram."

[10] (82) A good example of the twist in the tail and the humour of surprise. The first four lines present a reasonable enough picture, the nonsense image coming in the fifth and final line.

[11] (83) A good example of the deadpan commenting last line. I like this, but consider (128) even better. The understated last line of (4) is attractive.

[12] (86) Our higher centres of learning have contributed to the national repertory many more limericks than those included in this collection. Some are adaptations of limericks originally referring to other places and other people. But this seems the genuine thing, as does (90).

[13] (94) One hears similar stories, with varying counts, of old men, young and old women—clearly people have little to do in Peru.

[14] (97) A limerick of rare charm, the image lingering

long in the mind after its first entry.

[15] (113) A legitimate rhyming device, spelling out the word, as long as it is not overdone. See also (77).

[16] (169) Mr. Fletcher believed one should chew every mouthful of food thirty-two times before swallowing. People with ideas like that tend to get forgotten.

[17] (171) Bridlington, Yorkshire. A dialect adaptation. This dark eyed Italian had a similar success in Madrid.

[18] (180) The limerick of the cruel—but our emotions are disengaged by the nonsense, just as in *Three Blind Mice* and other nursery rhymes.

[19] (209) Attributed to James Joyce, who liked to cock a snook at the clergy now and then. But there is a cautionary note in Oliver St. John Gogarty's remark (Chapter XX, *As I Was Walking Down Sackville Street*) that he had "heard that not once or twice in our rough island's story." I have been told by one who knew Gogarty that he composed not a few limericks himself.

[20] (233) A good example of clever rhyming.

[21] (235) Another example of bright rhyming with the addition of a rhyming volley in the last line.

[22] (236) A brilliant limerick in which the star role is at times given to various Bishops and Mayors. If you want one in the eye for any figure of authority, just put in the name of your choice.

[23] (242) Compare Lear's:
> There was an old person of Anerly,
> Whose conduct was strange and unmannerly
>   He rushed down the Strand
>   With a pig in each hand,
> But returned in the evening to Anerly.

[24] (274) The pause, represented by the hyphen, can be effective in the limerick—as here.

[25] (290) Rossetti liked to poke fun at his contemporaries in limericks:

153

There was a dull painter named Wells,
Who is duller than anyone else;
    With the face of a horse,
    He sits by you and snorts—
Which is very offensive in Wells.

Where the limerick is concerned, bawdy is best. Arthur Wimperis wrote: "The only limericks in my experience of any literary merit are distinctly Rabelaisian. Beside these, the more polite examples fade away into the dim haze of mediocrity." Arnold Bennett and George Bernard Shaw expressed the same opinion.

[26] (299) In (147) one was prepared to give Alice the benefit of the doubt. But to repeat her misdemeanour in such a place is either malice or gross carelessness.

[27] (321) A fellow called Scott, who took a girl out in his yacht, behaved as abominably. One suspects he is one and the same person.

[28] (325) There is more than a touch of the nursery rhyme about this one.

[29] (327) Obviously the same chap as in (223), but an outside account. Very fair reporting, at that.

[30] (328) A vigorous verse, with lively rhyming.

[31] (340) Clearly American. The limerick, an Anglo-Saxon tradition, is just as popular in the United States as in Britain and the Commonwealth.

[32] (349) A neat twist to "The Faith Healer of Deal" (81).

[33] (355) *Excusado* is the Spanish for lavatory. One doesn't need to know that to appreciate this limerick; but it's well worth remembering if you visit Spain.

[34] (367) And why not? British plumbing is talked about the world over.

[35] (404) A vigorous verse that male readers will not treat too lightly.

[36] (410) It would have helped the rhyming volleyers if Titian had been a physician. Just a thought.

The first edition of the *Encyclopaedia Britannica* I consulted pointed out that the best limericks are "faultlessly dactylic throughout", and gives an example. But a more recent edition says that limericks are usually anapestic—which the previous example was anyway. Which just goes to show that you should rely on your ear for what is basically a simple verse form and not get ensnared in technical matters. In two words—*have fun* !

INDEX